Aflame

Aflame

Gary McDowell

The White Pine Press Poetry Prize

WHITE PINE PRESS / BUFFALO, NEW YORK

White Pine Press
P.O. Box 236
Buffalo, NY 14201
www.whitepine.org

The White Pine Press Poetry Prize, Volume 25

Grateful acknowledgment is made to the journals where these poems first appeared or are forthcoming, some in different forms:

32 Poems: "The Itch." *American Poetry Review*: "Sorrow from Far Away Is a Kind of Power." *The Bennington Review*: "History Repeats Itself, as Seen from My Hotel Room Window." *Booth*: "Long Hunter State Park, Late Winter." *Descant*: "Sometimes Spilled Spices on a Countertop Look Like the Night Sky." *Drunken Boat*: "The Lazarus Reflex." *Gold Wake Live*: "They All Chatter Mouthful." *Hotel Amerika*: "Suburbia" and "Miranda Rights." *The Laurel Review*: "Palindrome." *Linebreak*: "Entrance to the Underworld." *The Nashville Review*: "Marriage, Ten Years In." *The Pinch*: "Upon a Concussion" and "Prayer Is Not Asking." *Pinwheel*: "Reading Plath in Early April." *Third Coast*: "Binary Code." *Zone 3*: "Winter in Nashville" (as "Mariner")

Book design: Elaine LaMattina

Cover art: Andreii Muzyka

Printed and bound in the United States of America.

ISBN: 978-1-945680-40-3

Library of Congress number: 2020930088

If everything is receding
from everything, we're only
seeing the backs of the stars.

—Les Murray, "Big Bang"

Table of Contents

IV.

I.

Desire and Keep Quiet

We can later be convinced how to say *rose bush*,
buds the color of bruises fleshed deeply. The small

space of we, a chapel. It's dire in here. Twins
in the womb: Do they grow side by side or front

to back, and does it make a difference? Something
is happening the way grapes fermented the first time,

the air all around dilated. It is such a favor the fervor
of sundown. What was a blink once is now eight billion

miles: The origin of water on our planet. Why not
elsewhere from a cloud of dust, cold hydrogen. Without

time, he said. When you learn something, he said, learn it
right. My dad when I was a child bought me a telescope—

the general store kind—so we could see—not the neighbor
girl undressing, though it occurred to me more than once—

not the stars—because let's be honest, they are too far
and too dim—but maybe Mars or Jupiter when they snuck low

and unoccluded beneath, slid, really, bulbed and on fire.
The moon or the half we can see and maybe too Saturn's rings:

Ice and dust backlit like billions of snowflakes in a single
streetlight, impossibly dense. One time in a letter I wrote

to a woman I loved but wasn't dating I said I saw a shooting
star, but I hadn't seen a shooting star, at least not that night.

Other nights, in northern Wisconsin, I've seen them sheen
and scatter like so much confetti. Even the bats swooping

leather-winged over top the campfire couldn't distract
from the simmer above the pines. So much of what we see

is the trajectory of no light, and for a long time I used to love
the word *steeple*. For a long time I sought to join any church

that had one but soon realized the summit of any steeple
is lonely and I need fewer and fewer rituals. What does

miles-per-second feel like, what can we know of crossing
counties and cities and states of being in blinks of an eye less—

life is blameless. A friend called today to ask *How often do I*
water the spinach? Seeds or plants? I asked. *Seeds*, she said,

and it's still so cold, so long until they leaf, and I think of distance
and desire, the work each takes. Time and my love, a form

beside ourselves: Climb down, loop up the window. Here is the view.

Binary Code

If the house is on fire, say no.
　　　If during the rainstorm, a daughter,
　　　　　　sleepless, crawls into bed beside you,

say yes, say, *some light is better than none.* If
　　　before you a young man kneels,
　　　　　　drive a safe distance away, read

the sign above the interstate—*practice safe*
　　　text—and be at perfect peace, else
　　　　　　there are more than two ways

for *I can't* to become *I won't* to become
　　　I don't remember how. Remember how
　　　　　　the house smoldered, the rose bushes

charred like so many bulbs burned out,
　　　like so few roofs for so many upturned lives.
　　　　　　Be kind, but also be habitual, be the blown

kisses you pretend to catch barehanded,
　　　your smile so true that your jaw aches,
　　　　　　tired, consumed by what forever goes

unsaid: *We are in mourning.* Say it aloud so you
　　　can hear it: *We are in mourning.* Say it again
　　　　　　and perhaps you will believe it: *We are always*

in mourning. Say it, maybe in a mirror, your
　　　eyes open like mouths hungry: *We are never not*
　　　　　　in mourning. We are in mourning. Say it and mean it.

Be exhausted. There is no other way to be alive.

Sorrow from Far Away is a Kind of Power

Between the spider and the jailbird, between the lover and the poet,
between the friend and the body,
                                        I'll take the body

unfolded, the perfect ratio of grit to pillow.

This is the first time I have washed my body
since you touched my body.

I want to wake you: *I dreamed about the woods,* I'd whisper,
but you'd turn away, feign sleep.

This is the flat-Earth theory of love affairs
where space and chaos figure out

that coincidence is lonely.

You lie now on your back like a jigsaw,
like the wrong tool from the wrong toolbox,

worrying smooth with your fingers
                                        your ear lobes,
the porch lights drawing the lawn tightly around our home.

Tomorrow I will learn a theory so dense
it will send you into mourning:

Show me again how to take you home.

Miranda Rights

A squirrel, a sparrow—does it

matter?—cries stuck in the chimney.

All the birds in mourning stay

grounded. The empty space

between the click-on of the heat.

You sit in a body and think

of a body. *Fault*: The other side

of the distance between us.

This wind: The leaves break

into a single leaf and are sucked

through the valley your house

and their house make. The difference

between a mirror and an answer—

are shapes named for what

they resemble? This means

that the body stays inside the body

so long as you wound it quickly.

Jutting ribs or lantern paper:

Either way, *dazzling*, the ribbon

in your hair. Like evening, go out

and darken what hollow you find.

What If There Are Deer in the Afterlife?

You've seen the Northern Lights,
worn a wedding ring, been named

most-likely-to-carry-his-own-casket-
to-the-riverbed-unencumbered-

by-the-rain. All you can do is see:
In this, you even out time—

there's the before and the during
of the day you wore a Houndstooth

jacket, your hand turning over
the birch-wood door-handle.

Between silence and yes: The tinsel
of *deep in the house.* The old stoop

sings in the wind-storm, the dizzying
work of the yolk, no, the *yoke,*

the brilliant relief of *neither.* How deer
survive a brushfire: They become

an island, share a throat—or know
that atoms are nothing but the light

they return. The eavesdropping
required to weep. Of course, there is

no key, not even a map. It is morning
at last, and your answer, in lieu

of grass, is somewhere in every distance.

Upon a Concussion

I go out. The ice fractals underfoot, and I slip, loose my feet. I imagine
spine or ankle, the fracture a shadow forward racing makes. Light

and dark, that in-between, eclipse, lean into my body, frame me,
when my hands reach out to catch me. On my back, cold and sore,

the trees and windows background the barren, fussy geometry.
What filters through: How photons—*kiss me*—shuttle, and it begins

again this morning. Yet it's there, this beauty growing and beyond
fully waking, here I am, too. I am the overripe. Birds lift. The window,

the screen. Robins, their chests still burnt orange—*kiss me*—fight for seed.
To study their caresses, a lesson in what awaits recollection. This is

dawn, when no two birds look alike, but are all precisely the same
except their fatigue like a planet rising to light. There is no emergency

but to vanish into pieces: See the whole, slowly visible so far away.
The impossibility of absence staying still. A notch of blood down my

temple. I believe a little dance this early is never too narrow. A body
is one form of terror upon darkness. Animalistic, she'd said. *Kiss me,*

she'd said. Headache, a simple knotting and unknotting—*kiss me*. What
I hear versus what throbs in my ears. Kiss me. I try to stand, trust that

gravity will, in time, do the rest. Frost on the window diagrams lines
like the ones on my palms. Frost upon breath, upon breath—*kiss me*—

and this is what's so damn hard to understand: How space can shrink
when it's never not expanding faster than it ever has. Sour darkness,

a single day. What can fill you up exists in the wind's drumbeat—*it's cold,*
kiss me. My head against the siding, the knobby, the sway, the braided way

I can't fall asleep when the largeness is real. My eyes open. The flight
to the planets—*kiss me.* The wiring necessary for such lift. Knowledge

for the sake of knowledge versus the need to feel pain or pleasure. On
the power lines this morning, a squirrel ran full speed, stopped, turned,

ran back to its mate, nuzzled in its neck, and they then ran off together.
Kiss me if pace could be barren, if freckling. I scribble how two—*kiss me*—

bodies, overripe, restore the bluing, the opening of the horizon-line.
Now, *right here on the lips.* Unfold me, *kiss me.* Marry me, Daylight,

and I will buzz into your ongoingness. *Kiss me.* Or tell me how to turn away.

History Repeats Itself, as Seen from My Hotel Room Window

The horses that gallop overhead on the hotel

    Room wall brown-dust, unfurl—those beasts—

Into a connect-the-dots of whirl and prairie.

    They say exile begins at birth.

I want to say I understand but understand

    I don't want to say. When you board a plane,

Do you ever think: These may be the last

    Faces I'll ever see? How about when standing

On the corner (not) selling loosies? Or

    Walking through a park? In the street?

Fear is the difference between space and time

    If time is a stubborn fool. We must face ourselves

As we halve in half the light in us. Without

    Present, past, and future there's no consciousness—

We must hold them simultaneously like how our brains,

    As we shift our gaze across the room, suppress

Our vision. In order to compensate we assume,

Not unreasonably, that everything in the room

Is stationary. A nowhere tide. The news

Moves like this, too. Cherry Blossom Festival, Local

Fifth Grader Wins Science Fair, Police Shoot Unarmed

Man—a black man, a young black man, a black

Boy, a mother's child. Every night in November

Is darker longer than the last. Be merciful be

Kind be the flash snowfall makes under

The streetlight. Be in swallow, bait a man with

A promise of *furthermore*. We cannot muster. I'll

Have no part of things perennial—the purpose

Of time is to slow us down this downward

Roll we travel. The broad back of the carp I

Caught in the Fox River, the grunt and breath of it

As I unhooked from its lips the flash,

How milky its lips to touch though below

That flesh a great dam of bone. Once we

Have worked long in the sun to tear one

Thing from another, we might think we have

Proved the world beautiful. Proof beneath

The fires that burn down churches. A rubbed

Shadow. Truth begins when you say it's all

History. There's a backdrop: Flame in flame,

How the night can wear the moon, its

Mirror—there is no light here, only smoke,

Which is itself a map of the universe,

A pattern not unlike the way a voice can hang

Beside a body and go unheard. Not a sensation

But a repetition. Montgomery. Selma. Baton Rouge.

Even cicadas can pick the cotton. We've no room

For anymore, thank you. When we listen, we

Hear one chord at a time—it is only our sense

Of past and future that makes it a song.

Marriage, Ten Years In

Sometimes I wonder   what

the neighbors   wonder—

do they spin "At Last" on repeat until they fall

asleep? Have husband and wife

                                        agreed—or one agrees

and one gives in—to a trial separation? So delirious—she

sleeps inside the dog and he sleeps on the porch—

I would like my jealousy to become our secret.

What adjustments. The air conditioning, the dog—again—who

ate the bagels?   Please go upstairs. Please

go up the stairs—   Upstairs.

The villain the ghost the bad guy hides there

the suspicious noise the baseball bat under

your bed   but what do you hope

to do with it the….   *Honey, I heard*

something downstairs. Go see what it is—

This time you really aren't   alone—

And sometimes you then wake in a lakehouse—

buzz of locusts, not traffic, saw blades saw

blades.   Vertical call of the loon,

the affect of mourning doves. We all lose

sometime. Burrow—burrow here

                                    and dwell.

This is the tin can. This is the root. How

you heard the glass shatter, the crowbar crack

the deadbolt   *the*   *the*   *the had it*

coming—

                        Thighs as a reward but for their fire.

Liberation is less rout than a meandering coming

to. A tensile spinning out of. Flamed with lush

horror like when a lover pats your head. It's

not ever not over—

                        Tomorrow and another

morning. The neighbors roll the trash bin to the curb,

wave, retreat back into their garage—holiness

of routine, of waking early to

                                              unlearn

love and learn it—and each other—again.

II.

Aflame

I.

Sometimes we want to talk to someone—

you are a shadow saying, *let's make*

love in the early heat. You won't admit

the moonlight, and you tell me

to put the soul in the sleeper, to collect

two of every every curdling body.

II.

The thigh's hollow, the visible breath,

and you're perched at the bed's

edge. I'm pinioned and you say

you don't want to live here

anymore. Blurs the wind.

We are on the cusp, air from

your mouth like wing beats,

you don't get it. I'm the resident,

I'm the aloe. We're unspooling.

On all fours my pulse pummels.

I see a cavern, a rill, the slow

accretion of the dark dark. This

is primal, this is what blinds us

to fall onto our backs again

to swallow one another.

We are convenient

as the sun spills the room.

Watch, we've come here

only bodies and will leave consumed.

III.

Their nests may disintegrate, may turn black and ash

and broken like so many homes, but rarely are birds singed

—O to be winged—what I am confessing: My wife and I

at the kitchen table and I imagine I'm texting someone else:

What I'll do to you. You've never in your life. No one's ever talked

to me like this before. Tongue between your. Against the wall.

I don't tremble. I don't stutter. There are 360,000 house

fires every year. If ours burst into flames right now,

I wouldn't be surprised. Neither would I welcome it,

but I'm also not sure we'd escape out the same door. Trust

is incidental like a lick of fire up an oak's trunk.

IV.

We, like a stream of—we a mouth, and it comes:

Waiting is different from patience. We dusk, we fate,

the thickest ticking of our hands. How long

we've waited is long enough. We wait, we enough,

are we continuous? There is a doorway, make of it

a sound. The difference between falling and having fallen,

an acorn pressed fierce into my palm and a handful

of hip-flesh—two kids, so much pushing—

the thrust of *if you died, I'd be alone but never again so lonely.*

V.

Of course the deer in the road

last winter, its spirit a hive,

its hide a hive. The vultures'

heads steaming when they looked

up to watch us pass.

VI.

When on fire, only the spirit fights

harder than the body: The mutiny

we undergo when aflame. First,

the wildness, the running away. Then,

the rigidity—I've seen the pictures

in the firehouse's filing cabinet—

I worked there several summers, wrote

reports, looked at evidence—a succumbing.

It's not the burns that kill—so many

photos of dismantled bodies—it's

the lack of oxygen: The fire eats it all:

The fire wants to breathe more than you do.

VII.

Quietly—the stars: *Bright* doesn't do.

In order to make, heat. Curves to

linger. Nothing as quiet as lightning.

Our space here, carved. One is in

space *where only light seems to have pressed.*

We are lean and darkness hums.

Gone too, I cannot see—and then.

We ought to go to bed—

we are so much left to devour.

VIII.

She says, *The dog's ear is swollen*

or filled with——. Later, we learn

a new word. Together, our tongues

click it: *Hematoma,* and like that

the lyric happens: I'd like

to tie you a ribbon

around your wrists

behind your back and lay

you down. We stumble.

We don't do it like that,

you say. There is a way

to say marriage without this.

Beautiful in the cellar, beautiful

in the attic——how much

of you——I will put anything

in my mouth.

IX.

It's not who (started the fire) but how (the fire started).

Forest fires burn millions of acres per year. Fire worships

air, breathes, propels itself like we lavish praise with tongue

and fingers. It's not who you marry but how you worship.

I've got this wrong. There must be a means of egress.

—*fire*, from Old English *fyr*. Two roots: *Paewr*, inanimate,

fire as substance; *egni*, animate, fire as living force. Not

until 1500 was someone ever *on fire*, as in 'aflame.'

Seven people die every day in house fires and half of all

marriages end in divorce. How do the other half end?

X.

Like kicked dead leaves there's a hardness.

You and I doubled in the dark. It's that we've

grown—us our favorite beast. What I wanted

was to look up and watch your body unfold.

Before you, age and light, shoulders,

whispering, *please, but not right now.*

XI.

Little stones drink the moon, light a path

like glass to the sunflower rooted

beneath the birdfeeder. *Blossom* as an urge—

how rarely we confess our hands.

XII.

The lack of cleft for—in—

the body. The light through

my eyelids becomes less and less

the light it once was.

Darkness is better than pity.

XIII.

Fire isn't matter—it's a side effect of matter changing

form. Water is merely burnt hydrogen. We've landed

on the moon this way: Vapor, pressure, millions of pounds

of thrust. Did I stray? Two atoms combine to release

heat, often light. However briefly. We fucked like fire:

Effervescent, unplanned, spreading upward, we were

pointed at the top like a flame, like reentry, fierce.

And we end our story like it began: Who are we alone?

XIV.

I've faked a fever

for your hand to touch my brow.

The grass bristles

ankle-high. She and sun: We

gouge each other by what we

must look like—

only willows root near

enough the shore.

I call it longing.

You call it *empty is the barrel.*

XV.

What holds true for time holds true too

for fire: I comforted the fire with a stick—

I then fed the stick to the flames.

XVI.

I thought to carry you over

the threshold / my shoulder.

Drink this fervent, most beautiful.

The lemon tree glistens,

coaxed to fruit, humidity says.

Hope ferments

the edges, your dress

a lampshade now were I to tear it

off you fast enough.

I love you at a boil

where there's a fire.

We hose and soften

as a current.

XVII.

Elucidation was the first element discovered,

but Hydrogen is so much easier to understand—

if not an owl mask, then one gulp and you are

intoxicated. Night sweats and you are beautiful.

III.

Long Hunter State Park, Late Winter

No matter how fast I reach
      I can't catch the orange-throated
            lizard climbing the shagbark.

          He disappeared you! The logic
      my five-year old makes makes
me wish this kind of magic were real:

The lizard, brandishing a tiny
      wand, *ka-pooshes* me to where
            teleportation means she'll

            never age, means every day
      when I say, *You're up early*
today, and she says, *My dream*

ended and I had nothing else
      to dream, we're larger, another
            example of two bodies in

            orbit. Further down the path
      an oak's branches like fingers
lift a fir tree's skirt. A mosquito

but larger. A wristwatch fallen
      into the leafmold. The shade sheds
            into light. Even this canopy,

      holy, has an end.

Follow Me, Dear

Daughter.   Angle of witness.

The body's seasons   never rest.

In death.   In tongues.

The windows,   stalks of thyme,

marjoram   drifting bloom to bulb.

Fully-lined. A survivor but which survivor, stop,

never stop this trembling. Hand-in-

hand we walk backward envious of astronauts,

often

in the moonlight, God forbid—though no one

admits it—Yes—God forbid—

waiting. .   Will grow to be:

This afternoon an asteroid flew between

the moon   and the earth,

some 217,000 miles away—a close call

in cosmic terms   is a long shot

in any other terms.   A storyteller's

dilemma: There was once.

There is no more.   There must be again.

Thank God beauty is more clever than intellect.

We fall in love, we fall out of love, we have

mercy by mistake.   We pour, we poor,

we consume, we whistle.   Otherwise

salvation says, the other voice, a face inside—

the day tries itself.   What leaves

the body—I plant poppies. Sticky with pollen,

my daughter's fingers point without apology.

She's touched for the first time labor—

I'm the instant,   she's the voice—

(shhhhhhh).

What exhales? What if reconciliation, if this,

turns out to be the point?   Sculptures

of Hermaphrodite,   portraitures flourish.

The coming together of masculine and feminine, of stone

and stone.   My daughter doesn't need

protecting, we all need protecting.   Her name

is the basis.   Unions and fertility.

Remember all seeds start as—   I don't know

what seeds are, but they must start somewhere,

even

in the mind like light in an otherwise dark

room—here's a story: Even without me

she'll grow to supplant me. My waiting, my

watering. None of it will stunt. This revelation:

I was and have been,   though the world,

wishing her further to love that which cannot love her back.

The Lazarus Reflex

Starlings *name the sky, the skirt.* They swoon

and every one fills the twilight. A stuck leaf

or shoe-black in the moonlight: Grief's story

tells everything, and we wake the hill to climb

where the starlings circle. The lovely hang

of their wings, of a stranger—distance in waves—

as wind swings a swingset. Is it that color,

the sky, exactly? Painted, turned toward—

upward slightly—you are lying through

your sunset. O to be a fortune-teller. O

to make still. Voices, shadows, bodies—

the merit of a sculpture, of starlings.

A locked door, faces shaped like candles,

like memory hacking light, the Old English

word for *saw blade*, a snout, a thrashing river,

and we remember to rejoice in fever. Cross

your arms over your chest, measure the distance

between the wicker chair and the landfill,

and tell me, starling, that miracles never happen.

Sometimes Spilled Spices on a Countertop
Look Like the Night Sky

I.

Last night a power surge   a bang

then whimper   lights on   lights—darkness

again   and then quiet. We learn

later that a transformer blew, shocked 10,000 of us

into *look at the stars how bright.* My wife and I,

kids asleep,   read by candle-

light—   When we evolved to language,

our bodies   our brains   suddenly required more sleep.

Before, when we fought to tear each other's bodies down, we slept

quickly, eager to pulse and eat and walk. And fight and bleed

for land for power, and then: Culture. Sometimes

I worry the soul will never catch up to the body.

II.

Every time my daughter sees   a butterfly,

an exclamation! There's no need for *species, genus,* is it bad

is it good. Just *butterfly.* Quantum mechanics tells us

something is everything and nothing simultaneously.   For instance,

a pair of gloves.   Once observed,

one is the right-hand glove and the other is the left-hand glove,

but in the moments before they are observed, before they

have glove-ness—before *space is sewn together*—

both gloves are left- and right-handed. And one isn't

the other   until the other is defined.

Einstein called this *spooky action at a distance.*

III.

I call it thickening, a   thing permitted,

gleaming, understood

(though we read for over an hour, our eyes soon tired,

and our hands   suddenly awake

(once a couple marries, scientists observe a decrease in passionate love

and an increase in deep attachment. This enables them

the longevity needed as a couple to raise children)

we fell until the morning blanched our shades—

she came I came she came I came I came I came—

there's a lesson to be learned here,

but I don't know yet what it is—)

                                                    like song

brought forth, an acceleration   of feeling.

Fatherhood. I am tired.   A child's

fist.   A child's

fist in my own.   *Where has she always been?*

Here.   Beside herself.

IV.

There's no way back. She's told

no   and becomes

indignant. *Are you mad at me?* she asks often enough that I doubt

myself. Was I too stern? How else to learn—

like this we come to appreciate one another's gravity—

we orbit, but give and take—   There is

a center, a hinge, but none of us can admit it's there—

or the illusion—

the salt and pepper and paprika and thyme—ends

before we can believe it. She's learned now to roll

her eyes, and the circles they make   like a moon

will move more men   than will conquer her.

First Image of the Moon

Shoot and hope, they said, it might be easier.
What totems, the firsts of anything. The glass

of water on my nightstand throws curved blades
of light: To understand what fields and fluxes

exist between—of what is light composed?—until
I knock over the glass and all the contained spills

out. There are always so many surprises in the night.
Between restful or restless sleep, the difference.

I want a new use for myself, a fugue, something
mindless. Passive observation from the surface

was all we had for millennia: What great rock and sky
of milk, of marble. What of mist and ruby when

the clouds flood. My hands are two things in my pockets.
The Greek word for planets means *wanderers*,

and the Romans named them after their deities. They
didn't blink like stars, were dependably in the same

spot every year on the same day. What they had was facility.
The morning gem of Venus, or our moon, its bright,

the hollow, the yellow mossy sky, its sinew—how nearly
with forceps pinched between fingers and one eye closed

you could pluck it, hinge it into your hands. The first six
missions failed. Imagine the very idea of unmanned

lunar pictures: Even when grainy we thought it spectacularly
white, the ridges, though, like worn asphalt, dark, its crust

formed through fission, the pressure of Earth's gravity.
It is our shield. She—for she is a she because she protects—

lends her sleep to the shape of love, lives another kind
of life, and I look up—I'm always only ever waking up,

sprouting—waiting for wonder like falling snow, limbs
Numbed: Nature is unwavering. I become time, I become

time's shadow so as to pilfer from there, from up there,
thousands of miles above the small blue voice, the long

curiosity of light. That seed, that idea: To see it close, closer,
suddenly close enough like the morning after, to nearly

touch it. Scientists tell us that an auditory event appears
longer than a visual one in our memories, in time, and so

our cheers and congratulations outlast the thing we
celebrate. Every time we tell a story it changes: We call this

beauty, we call this love: My grandmother knits you a sweater.
We are sometimes, perfectly sometimes, a little windy,

but the moon is a differentiated body built from fire
and force—we should welcome eternity on a good morning.

It is impossible to remember anything when we have no news
worth the confusion, and that's when it becomes more and more

apparent that light has nothing to do with darkness, is so simple to touch.

The Itch

Each day a day to hide in. Overhead, the geese
coax the other geese South: How is it that they

find their way? The long touching of their voices,
the trailing behind of their mates: The sound

their wings make like an engine idles, a bucket
of coal dust dropped to a thud. A cave in the middle

of the night. To know migration is to know life
the hard way. *The doctor will see you now.* This is

the whirlwind since we've been together: Stunted
by our rending. The leaves have fallen. You, wife,

are sleeping—how do your hands work independent
of one another. Is the cloudlessness a symptom?

Or. One answer is that I know how to lie to myself.
Everything will be okay. I can walk on water, but I

don't because I remember that I haven't before—
instead, moonlight, instead, thunder like a hymn,

a resonant thrumming: *Peace be with you. And with you.*
Trust me the way one animal thrusts into another,

and this too yields toward long ago gratitude. We are
nothing if we aren't waiting for the apocalypse, my

darkened-eyes. We were so young then. What causes
pain? What cures it? What parts of you may I touch?

Whispers are dazzling, love. We were hungry for ourselves,
and now for salt, for bands of weather, for a frontier

I wish to carry you toward.

Reading Plath in Early April

The box is only temporary.

The bees gallop—no, that's not right—the bees
won't stray from—the bees' astonishing delay—the bees

turning back—the most perfect passage—they take
place, I mean, in the world as it thickens—they have

their way—misdirection, like spring, is a turning—the bees
in each firm beginning—the bees loom, stub—the bees—

every indiscretion—the bees render—twisted into hollowed
tree trunks, in nests underground, we find them always

when we least expect to—the bees look alike—bend the branch
down to set them reeling—they know no better—their

stinging is solitary work—the bees' every single note—
the hive is a circuit board—the bees, as a child I thought

the bees, their stingers, could stitch, make small leaps up
or down my arm, plunge plunge plunge—the bees, though,

sputter through—the eye is most ours when shut—the bees
find all they want—come with me—they collapse too.

First Celestial Body

Logic like time like stars has no backdoor,

    knows only one direction. As with praying,

      I don't know where to start. She wrote: it feels

better *if my eyes are pressed shut*, because so much

    escapes vision. The view of two oceans

    simultaneously. Am I alone? Dawn about to move

let me forget. I lift again my hands to lace

    my fingers—prayer is the mouth of the singer

    muted. I crack open his door, my son, to remember

light, how even it can fail. I read once

    that a certain kind of grasshopper glows in the dark.

    Or maybe it was a jellyfish. Their bodies—like a boy's

in sleep—static but dreaming. For the young.

    I watch until he puts his feet to the floor and is awake.

    He will not stop until again he dreams. Why do people

do cruel things? We hope our neuroses are not

    pathologies. We pass down a moment's work, but

    imagination, things divine. Surviving a funeral, a coffin

borne by youth. Subtlety is a lifelong pursuit. *I wish*

    for you what I wished before, but harder. Betrayal and eggs

    and lard. . .skip this and the interwoven poplar trees out back,

how their limbs clap together high above the ground,

    the wind its own theatre. *If destruction be our lot,* said a wise

    man. How do we survive survival, the aftermath that's new?

      [1959. Russia. The first humans to see,

to know the other side, and the crater, dark

and deep that faces us, the Sea (of Tranquility),

delivered via feed, slowly, the men

in the control room ate fish bones, cold

broth, were our only shade against a war

we didn't understand. Stealing, drinking

like beasts disputed with fists, their own

urine, to be seen, then only enough

saliva. Finally rain saved the well. So

scarce: *Your house I spend the day.*

If you don't like the sea.]

Of course it's the birds that hear me, eyes and herds

and clusters, the idea side of faces. We aren't infinitely

present ever you've a twin identical down to it's the body

that refuses understanding until something makes

sense. There's so much I want to tell you, son, that you

aren't ready to hear. There are ugly deaths and then there

are the already dead. You who grew up in a movie version

of a storm, underlings and cowards, your parents' war lapping

at your feet, on TV, images of the sea and the Sea that hangs

like a painting you can't reach through the glass case

from your stroller, *Daddy, it's so big and it's so far away.*

Someday your father will lay to rest after his body.

He will be the color of your dead father. Heart failure

while your mother in a suburb where no houses stand empty

there will be now an empty house, and is, and is, and I'm sorry.

Entrance to the Underworld

My boy wants to dig to the other

side—   Of what, I

ask.   To where people are.

How come the moon some days is visible

in the afternoon?   What refraction,

what luminosity. Miles down, what's there

at the bottom   of the Earth?

What's there at the center   Some questions

with answers aren't worth answering. His imagination

seized—is there a center? He thuds and thuds the dirt

with a spade. I think we're close, he says. He looks

away, then back again   to the dirt.

Does he know

his time is coming? Does he know, the minutes barbed

now, the day years from now when he realizes

there is no center—   (or is there?)

I understand that sometimes by looking for something

we invent it: Thus one definition

of *truth*, one version

of *vision*. I read that the desire to breathe

is our most primitive urge. How loyal we are to what

contains us   though we narrow

toward something finite   or vice versa.

Orange was a fruit before it was a color. When

we were kids, we found

                         a jawbone in the back-

yard. Explorers. Discoverers. The shoulders of giants, we thought

the Earth had opened   her secrets to us,

and maybe she had. History, like poetry, knows nothing

of narrative but is charged   with the now.

Everything we touch turns into a downspout. The tree parallel

to where my son digs dropped at my feet last fall

a sparrow's nest, eggs still unhatched. The mother,

distraught or scared or—had never seen such a thing—

wait   I can't know what she

thought   or even if she did.

Mourning, like desire, is light followed by fits of

astonishing darkness—one a hole you climb into,

the other   a hole you fall into,

both, like the shadow a ladder casts against the side

of the house, never end, but extend forever. I ask

my son if he ever has nightmares.   What's a nightmare?

It's a new kind of closeness, an empty house with a boy

in it. A bear drunk on fermented berries, precisely

how we marvel at his heft. What we get for caring.

A river near and far—the unsaid, close, closer. We

cannot muster   what we've lost.

Sometimes I have nightmares with my eyes open.

IV.

By Age Sixty, We Lose 200,000 Things

Our sense of duty, if we're lucky.
    The Greeks didn't have a word for blue:

The *wine-dark,* they called it. The sea.
    Our keys. Skyward toward the plains

is a failure of imagination. If we can't
    name it, does it exist? Once upon

a time, the Earth was flat because
    we didn't know any better. Once upon

a time, the most kissed face in the world.
    Our souls. *Our souls*: You can't say

we didn't warn you. Cicadas every
    seventeen years, a brood is a brood

but we all know their hard shells
    are murderous to beauty, impenetrable

and visible as pinpricks as they spiral
    from the treetops to entangle your hair.

Our options. Spiritual error. Our options.
    One inside another inside another,

we squeeze out of ourselves the shade
    caught brilliantly in the corners. Have

you ever slept in an attic, the way the light
    both contains and illuminates, the shutters

maybe clasped or loosened, your rhythm
       the rhythm of last year's holiday lights

banging against the gutter. Our timing.
       How nothing, once churned, ever ends,

how what continues—our minds—continues
       even when out the window darkness comes.

Prayer Is Not Asking

What will not come undone? My head
in my hands to pray. I can't see what there is

to see. But to have eyes as mirrors otherwise
taking down what is visible. Looked at long

enough, bits of starlight produce coherent figures,
some ill-defined center. I shall begin I shall

stand I shall touch I shall note, and I see you now,
tiny reflection, in the linoleum. How new stars are

the death-throes of former stars, all of them millions of years
old, he said on the porch. The light, he said, you see

was born long before you and me and everyone else
altogether alive and maybe ever alive. And to think

the mission—to extend exploration beyond our
neighborhood, beyond the sun's sphere of influence,

beyond outer planets and limits, possibly beyond beyond.
The plump cardinal at the feeder is sick, never grazes

at night alone or with his love when they nuzzle,
and I can't go somewhere other than this body. How do

they know the heliosheath, the outermost layer
where the solar wind slows? What else these boundaries?

Interstellar particles and waves for the first time,
what does it mean to see truly what we've never thought

to understand? What existed yesterday but can't
tomorrow. Even at its current speed, even trajectory,

even fuel: The brightest star we can see is 40,000 years away,
is why the body grows accustomed, sustained by one note

hummed in a vacuum, one pinprick of light—or hope of one—
the lull and bright and think of it all, the space out there

between our hands, and this is our home now. Pair it
with rising and bending and own this lullaby that takes us there.

Palindrome

On our backs planning envy.
The two of us in secret always,

quietly our lips, censoring
the good sense to fall

in love. How you dream your
religion, your midnight human,

but that I'm a part of how you
vowel, your tongue soft against

the roof of your mouth against
my fingers taken deep against.

This year, we keep winter,
meaning each other, company.

We aren't up in the mountains.
But last night, the clatter, our bodies.

Church

"When God is a father, he is said to be elsewhere.
When God is a mother, she is said to be everywhere."
—Jenny Offill, *Dept. of Speculation*

I've always wanted   to build

a collection—not to own it   but

to compile it. Maybe of letters to someone I'll never meet.

A friend tells me he dreams that his eye

doesn't fit   in his eyelid

anymore.   A dream like a prayer begins

               as an urge.   An urge

to flee? What can resolve

itself only in darkness. On the way back from

an idea   of art   another urge—

what will it be like to *be* a corpse. Once I

watched a mouse   crawl into the bathtub,

and I didn't save it from drowning. When we say

disappear   we mean

there's a mirror.   Out the window

this iron fence,   fleur de lis,

the balcony only inches wide.   Who

rests there?

                              What.

You've a tattoo on your wrist.   Fleur de lis.

In the news.   more lately: *To become*

radicalized.   When

the body makes concessions.   The throat-burn

of bourbon. A helicopter.   An illusion   of low
skies,

noises, small feet on the ground.   Have you

ever seen a ghost?   Without environmental change,

complex forms of life cannot evolve—   chickens

lay more eggs when the days   are longer

in the summer.   Newborns synchronize

their movements to the human   voice—

what I'm trying to say:

                    Think of what's never   seen—

linger there like a submissive's tongue lingers. What's never

seen is never what's unseen: When you were a child,

dust in the sunlight   meant

speak softly   in your mouth.

Suburbia

Theory, a new home.
      No longer anonymous,
neighborly. In the street.
      Permits, scaffolds, barriers:
A burnt-out pilot light or two makes
      no difference. Embrace

in public at your own risk.
      The surest sign of the
(less degraded) status of this
      legislation for streetlights,
curfews, social like
      our century, our police,

by which we are read
      our rights, decree the blurring
of trends into patterns.
      Especially dire? What's inside
the black bodies of black men is
      what's inside my body,

I know, but I'm told our bodies, on corners,
      on sidewalks, in daylight:
We balance, make parades, hold hands,
      say we'll change.
The problem is that we don't know
      what to do with ourselves.

We say *unite, fight back*, this will be
      the moment. Horticulturists,
students, sack carriers, fathers, sons,
      or worse. I take a bath
tonight, see only the contour
      of my half-drowned body

in the dark and fogged mirror
       and think *lullaby,* think *I'm never*
only visible. Why into such perfect
       quiet do I let in the noise
I can't quiet alone? Who can be alive
       today and accept tomorrow?

They All Chatter Mouthful

My daughter's hand: How I know God is. The blackberries climb
the trellis as I climb from sleep. The dog is still and looks

at something. The maple out front is and is looked upon in the near
distance, from a certain angle, so steep, a vulture and a hawk soar

alike, but up (close enough to catch) a glimpse of tail forked
and the hover more hopeful, less shudder. My neighbor suffered

a head injury, and when he wakes, his brain can't tell his limbs
where they are in space. It's not like the falling dream, he says,

but worse, like being tangled in a curtain and spilled forth without
warning. What we hope for is the same as privilege. How soon

is too soon to misunderstand? We hung a hummingbird feeder outside
the back door. My daughter swears she can hear their wings. Humming-

birds can tell (or keep) time: A flower replenishes its nectar in twenty
minutes, so the birds know to go back, to satiate, before others catch

on. Differently, we'd call this (wings ablur) (the only bird that can fly)
backwards thinking or plot. I don't know how to be fearless, though

I'm pretty sure there's no such thing. Are we endlessly moving toward
the future or is the future coming toward us? Birds too often are a thing

that happens in the trees (through the backyard). The trees look too
pressed for time: What is it that they fight against that I from my (I circle

them) window can't see? One (I will watch them) again and two (I will
lay down among them). Forget what I said about the future. All my poems

are for my kids. They see me shadow and pass, her little hands in mine,
and my son's, too. Look, there's the moon out early today, though a storm

blows in. To go back inward, and then you'll hear it underneath the wind.
One birdcall unlike the others. What was it about birds again? That no

two look alike but they all chatter mouthful? I'm not scared of much:
The vultures predict their next meal and circle overhead: Carrion

from the Greek for *virtuous to find*, and now I'm lying. No matter how
Fast light travels, the darkness is always there first. Those of faith see time

as evidence. How streetlights click on at dusk. The bite of humidity,
and the neighbor's van blocks the driveway. On the news, an Ohio boy

talks of a woman named Pam, claims to have been Pam in a past life.
He is five years old and knows how twenty years earlier Pam died

leaping from a building to escape fire. Scientists claim consciousness
is the result of our being able to distinguish past, present, and future,

but what happens when the past becomes the present and the future ceases.
The idea of history: You can hear the click. Look up: There is hope yet. Her

little hand in mine, across my cheek. Even the nightlight is bright enough
to see by. I won't ever leave here. There was yesterday and today and tomorrow.

The resorting, the whispering, the please daddy right here, I'm right here,
I was here before you, and will be here after. The robin, the dove, the blue jay.

Don't Shoot the Messenger

Kneel when the siren, knees to chest, hands behind
your neck—this is safety the world over. I went

to a pond today to see where the water was stillest.
Near the far shore a young woman walks alone,

around shape as cover, willow and oak. The end
of the day was still far off: I've never been a victim.

I look up to spring's first robins unwrapping, unfurling
in yet leaved branches and droopings, their crowns

browner than dusk. It is five o'clock and still lit,
the clouds not notched into place, the stalks. The woman

smiles, says hello, she says. She has a dog, a white
and brown dog with paws too small for its legs like a candle-

stick in its pillar. You don't survive because you shoot
the messenger—you survive because you can't be unborn

like an atom splits. The splinter in your thumb you cannot
dig loose. It is time, they said, that the future have a face:

There is a hurry to arm ourselves. I lean down to pet the white
and brown (terrier) (immortal soul), and its tongue finds

my palm, and I kneel. Someone observing us from Andromeda,
our nearest neighboring spiral, would today see the Earth

of pre-Homo Sapiens, hunched primates making crude
stone tools in sub-Saharan Africa. Light can only travel

so fast, but observation happens immediately. The white
and brown licks my cheek—*this is the force* of meaning

what you say. No story *in the meantime* means it's still
spring until it's summer and then: Our attic gets so hot

and bodies have no refuge, though even a breeze can feel
like freedom—you're right, I can't believe I just said that.

I don't know her name. I notice her skin is not the same
color as mine and I am petting behind the ears of her white

and brown, so should I be ashamed to notice? I'm kneeling
and the sun casts a halo, a lighted shadow, where her face

just was. Her face is no doubt still there. Are scars—which are
a kind of expanse (tomorrow's, like a verb)—so deep? She knows

I know where we will go after this, but not together. New leaves will
come soon—how dare I speak for her?—to keep us looking up.

A kayaker floats further and stops paddling (look up) and it
becomes more and more apparent: We migrate. It takes a long time

to become a human being. The kayaker runs ashore and the white
and brown takes issue, takes refuge behind the woman. She tells

me *he's all bark* and I interject *and no bite*. Immediately I
understand a thing about dust motes in a certain slant, warmongers

and racial divides, and I let her voice in until the first hot breeze.
The white and brown's spit. Nothing can be universal and not

be divine. It's suddenly clear that I know nothing about myself, and
across the pond a boy and a girl fly a kite, their squeals distant at first

and then joyful, so joyful, and the woman smiles, *looks like fun,*
she says, drifting away, the brown and white, unleashed, I see,

though I didn't notice it before, races ahead, and I reach out
to touch her hand. If you give something away, you don't lose it.

Winter in Nashville

If boredom, as Heidegger argued, is the awareness
of time passing, is another word for the flyby between

our own existence and everyone else's, then it is also
the difference between that pothole and a dented wheel.

We like the truth and its edges, the bags in which we carry
our goods. What is passing before us in an arc—we swing—

and evening always comes, blooms, blooms. The evening
news says Mars is in retrograde and Venus last transited

the sun in early 2012, won't again while we're alive. No
one worries to be born again, newly named. Spring is

always coming next, can come sooner every year. Leaves
want to bud, and life finds its way back, and for an instant

we believe we understand the green, how wind picks its way
through those reeds—that field of failed wheat, is it all just atoms

colliding, some vision we fail to see through? How do we bear
not knowing? Given enough time, he says, life is inevitable.

Just wait—the future is always longer than the past, he says,
even though the present can end at any time. The fluctuations

that make us are minimal like the difference between touch
and caress. Tell me you've seen, near the end of a day, deeply

before rest, the opening of light onto a field of wild grass,
a bird or two settle itself into *a minute-ago*. This moment is

never a replica. You can choose to see it tonight, but you can
also choose to have seen it last night. Space appears infinite,

the billow and break of it. We are in wonder, so easy to miss
that which is invisible: *The only reason for time is so that everything*

doesn't happen at once. The sun orbits the Milky Way every
quarter-billion years and so our nearness to our neighboring stars—

I'm enamored with coincidence. Dear Echo, can you hear me
becoming me? I whispered so you could. An apology or a home:

Who says these are two different ideas? Math is the real language
of romance. The sun is so massive that it could, in theory, act

as a *telescopic lens* could we harness its light. Contradiction
is one of mankind's greatest inventions. Leave the door ajar,

that hardwood floor like a dirty mirror. If being flexible, if being
current, a gush of atoms underneath. Sometimes mystery is more

accurate than science. If the mirror, if the speed of glance over
the body: So much time passes. We bulge, I remember sight

in unison, boredom in the beholder. If we call the day *look*
at this place. If let us glory, I love you everywhere. Back

to worrying deeper holes. Again the margin for error—how
soon how long. It's so easy to fall in love with the wrong—

if impossible—mouth. My mouth on your thigh what wings
can carry us higher where we can be whole again.

The Stars and Our Response

We are roaring
        through the spaces
between the
        spokes, we are
the nails
        nailed to the sky
when something
        like a bat
swoops into
        view.
To be there
        when I sit
counting
        the leaves
of clover,
        or dancing
with my wife
        on heart-pine
flooring.
        The only
sound
        from the bats
is how they
        shade
the light
        from the moon,
a language
        with no name:
Unlike other
        animals, we
were made
        to stand
erect so

       we could
gaze at
       the stars.
We are
       cubes of light
that equal
       one another—
there are days
       when three
dimensions
       are three
too many,
       and those days
when we
       are larger
inside
       than out.

Author's Note

I'd like to thank Sean Thomas Dougherty both for selecting *Aflame* for The White Pine Press Poetry Prize and for his good words about it. Thank you, dear poet.

To Dennis Maloney, Elaine LaMattina, and the rest of the White Pine Press family: I'm incredibly honored. Thank you.

Matthew Guenette: You saw in this book something I didn't—and you saw it at a tabletop bar in Tampa, FL. I love you, brother. Thank you.

My brothers and sisters on the heart's road: Alex Lemon, Keith Montesano, Susan Finch, Amy Newman, F. Daniel Rzicznek, Traci Brimhall, and Erika Meitner. I love you all.

Thank you to Belmont University for the support given me to finish this book.

And as always and forever: Manz, Bubba, and Bug. You're everything.

The Author

Gary McDowell is the author of a collection of lyric essays, *Caesura: Essays* (Otis Books/Seismicity Editions, 2017) and five collections of poetry including, most recently, *Mysteries in a World that Thinks There Are None* (Burnside Review Press, 2016) and *Weeping at a Stranger's Funeral* (Dream Horse Press, 2014). He's also the co-editor of *The Rose Metal Press Field Guide to Prose Poetry* (Rose Metal Press, 2010). His poems and essays have appeared in journals such as *American Poetry Review*, *The Southern Review*, *The Nation*, and *Gulf Coast*. He lives in Nashville, Tennessee, with his wife and two children and is an associate professor of English at Belmont University.

THE WHITE PINE PRESS POETRY PRIZE

Vol. 25: *Aflame* by Gary McDowell. Selected by Sean Thomas Dougherty.

Vol. 24: *Our Age of Anxiety* by Henry Israeli. Selected by Kathleen McGookey.

Vol. 23: *Secure Your Own Mask* by Shaindel Beers. Selected by Alan Michael Parker.

Vol. 22: *Bread From a Stranger's Oven* by Janlori Goldman. Selected by Laure-Anne Bosselaar.

Vol. 21: *The Brighter House* by Kim Garcia. Selected by Jericho Brown.

Vol. 20: *Some Girls* by Janet McNally. Selected by Ellen Bass.

Vol. 19: *Risk* by Tim Skeen. Selected by Gary Young.

Vol. 18: *What Euclid's Third Axiom Neglects to Mention About Circles* by Carolyn Moore. Selected by Patricia Spears Jones.

Vol. 17: *Notes from the Journey Westward* by Joe Wilkins. Selected by Samuel Green.

Vol. 16: *Still Life* by Alexander Long. Selected by Aliki Barnstone.

Vol. 15: *Letters From the Emily Dickinson Room* by Kelli Russell Agodon. Selected by Carl Dennis.

Vol. 14: *In Advance of All Parting* by Ansie Baird. Selected by Roo Borson.

Vol. 13: *Ghost Alphabet* by Al Maginnes. Selected by Peter Johnson.

Vol. 12: *Paper Pavilion* by Jennifer Kwon Dobbs. Selected by Genie Zeiger.

Vol. 11: *The Trouble with a Short Horse in Montana* by Roy Bentley. Selected by John Brandi.

Vol. 10: *The Precarious Rhetoric of Angels* by George Looney. Selected by Nin Andrews.

Vol. 9: *The Burning Point* by Frances Richey. Selected by Stephen Corey.

Vol. 8: *Watching Cartoons Before Attending A Funeral* by John Surowiecki. Selected by C.D. Wright.

Vol. 7: *My Father Sings, To My Embarrassment* by Sandra Castillo. Selected by Cornelius Eady.

Vol. 6: *If Not For These Wrinkles of Darkness* by Stephen Frech. Selected by Pattiann Rogers.

Vol. 5: *Trouble in History* by David Keller. Selected by Pablo Medina.

Vol. 4: *Winged Insects* by Joel Long. Selected by Jane Hirshfield.

Vol. 3: *A Gathering of Mother Tongues* by Jacqueline Joan Johnson. Selected by Maurice Kenny.

Vol. 2: *Bodily Course* by Deborah Gorlin. Selected by Mekeel McBride.

Vol. 1: *Zoo & Cathedral* by Nancy Johnson. Selected by David St. John.